The 3:15 Experiment

**Bernadette Mayer, Lee Ann Brown,
Jen Hofer, and Danika Dinsmore**

The Owl Press • Woodacre, California • 2001

Acknowledgments:

Lee Ann Brown:
August 14 and 18 first appeared as "Definitions at 3:15" in <u>Polyverse</u>
(Sun & Moon Press, 1999)

Danika Dinsmore:
August 2, 29, and 30 were first published in <u>Traffic</u>
(It Plays In Peoria Press, 1996)
August 13 was first published in <u>Jackstraw Writer's Anthology,</u>
(Jackstraw Productions, 2001)

Special thanks to Danika for her continued enthusiasm and help with this project

Cover drawing "3:15" by Will Yackulic 2001

This first edition printed July 2001 at
Alonso Printing, Hayward, California

Typesetting by ROSE Inc. Forest Knolls, California

ISBN: 0-9669430-3-1

The Owl Press
P.O. Box 126
Woodacre, California 94973

www.theowlpress.com

The Owl Press books are distributed by Small Press Distribution,
Berkeley, California. www.spdbooks.org

3:15

INTRODUCTIONS

What's this humming in my skull, this diffuse crackling numbing the hour? What's this thought continuum loping around in my brain pooling forth in florid dream? I hear four women, pens outstretched in spontaneous gowns of song, sculpting my drowsy head afresh, writing and singing time to a pulp. Ahh yes, beauty— arise then, and listen!

I came across "The 3:15 Experiment" in June of 1999 in Boulder, Colorado under the tent at Naropa University, a thunderstorm keeping time to this panel of four women (or was it three? Jen I think was in Mexico)— Danika Dinsmore, Lee Ann Brown, Bernadette Mayer, and Jen Hofer (in spirit). The topics of their panel included time, consciousness (altered), collaboration, community, and ritual. I wanted to know, hear, read, more. As it turned out they were planning to open the experiment up to whoever wanted to participate, and were passing around a sign-up sheet. I excitedly signed my time away for the following August when the experiment would begin again. That year they changed the writing times to 12:00 noon and 12:00 midnight to accommodate the numbers of new participants. I wrote twice a day for almost the whole month. Discipline as always was an issue, and yet time, in a constant with its claws in my back, kept reminding. By the end of August that year twenty some-odd people had participated— a web site was made, history changed, time was humbled in our wake, and we with it. I knew then a book needed to be made with the four original and most consistent participants. And when I finally received the manuscripts spanning seven years and several time zones, I was irresistibly delighted by the impassioned reverence for that middle hour of 3:15— how it so wonderfully bloomed forward the raw truth no matter how groggy the writer— all in the form of no form, all in the form of dream drenched poem, in the form of eclectic song, of emotional "journaling" (you'll forgive the expression), of prosaic pop commentary. Each entry equally capable of reconfiguring your poetic clock, and bringing you back to the wide-eyed instant, the irrepressible moment, the divine urgency of the "here and now" in all its raw beauty. Throughout the text it is never a question of "if I have time", but rather when I *make* time for the "eternal present" all foreseen limitations dissolve. So wake up folks, and read! Wake up and write! Wake up and live!

—Albert Flynn DeSilver May 20, 2001 3:15 A.M.
Forest Knolls, California

The 3:15 Experiment has transformed throughout the years in attempt to keep things new. but the ideas of ritual, of collective consciousness, of altered states, and of record have remained. the first year we all wrote at 3:15 AM no matter where we were. over the next few years we adapted it for different time zones so we were writing simultaneously (i.e. 3:15 EST would be 12:15 PST). at one point we wrote twice a day, at midnight and noon. and in 2000, we went back to our original impetus, to wake and write at 3:15 AM. to see what 3:15 mind looked like...

what is time an empty bottle said. at the moment no one awake, alone yet busy with thought and dream and remembrance. recapturing day and making mental lists. putting it all in order with a lack of order. shuffling through. picking moments to explore. it is a comingness in sleep you can't pay attention to at any other time. and the ritual becomes a rhythm, so much that one sometimes wakes for days after at 3:15 because the body (and mind) has been trained to do so. the writing is by hand and often in the dark. no telephone or radio or tv or letter. observing what night brings and being one, part of, others. a dance. it is autopilot sometimes, reading over, at the end of the month it seems as if a far away voice were dictating and i simply transcribing without thought or opinion.

turn everything down and off, here in the middle of ritual it's something trans-dimensional. thought / prayer / song / dream / soft landing / moment / there / memory, yes, that's what i meant to say / i certainly like to look / bridges to jump off of / holes to crawl into / …

at 3:15, world slows, mind opens to impulse, direction, wandering.

a ritual in the middle of the night is a useless / useful thing. as i sit down, no, i rarely sit down to it, it is more a rolling over, shaking off some sleepy demon, something crawls up. it is what the day brought, what the dream brought and what is right in front of. there is more room at 3:15 to let this all in. process encompasses getting off of wherever i am and roving. never try to create anything, let it create itself from me and what is around me. and, remind myself that there are others up at the same time, everywhere, not just writing at 3:15, some writing and not realizing they are a part of it, some nowhere near writing, some pained, some delighted, some on the verge of birth or death (the many forms of) and this, too, is my birth and death. birth, as in: letting something new live, death, as in: as soon as something is written down it dies a little, it becomes recorded and never enough so, one can never record properly... *we are all pitiful historians*

what attracts me to ritual is the rhythm of the drip. half-conscious interior / exterior. is the partnership between self and other. the timelessness of dream-state. looking back on, looking forward to, and being simultaneously involved in the work. habits are hard to break. there is sadness in the middle of the night. the realization of utter aloneness there is pleasure in exploration. there is determination in getting it all down there is senselessness and the importance of senselessness. urgency. time to reflect in time. there is camaraderie in commitment there is tick, tick, tick. there is going back to bed after a task there is un/subconsciousness... that solidity of everything from nothing.

—Danika Dinsmore April 3-9, 2001 3:15 AM

Accurate Inaccuracy, A Certain Uncertainty, A Certain Unexpected Something In The Middle Of A Night

Sentences make and unmake slowly.
Sentences make slowly and unmake.
The city at night an entire city of sounds.
And resistance.
Superar - to overcome - the obstacle it is to sit up.

The past an act in present tense, often what I wanted to say or thought so forgets so uttering becomes itself in a process of distraction as time works laterally and kaleidoscopically, against measure. At 3:15 one tends to feel a sense of permission, to use a word like "time." Often the sound of violins, dogs or asphalt floats in. The city entirely a city at all hours and its melodies perhaps less knotted, though also less reliable, at such an hour. It is our other selves, our under-selves, who function in the night. Deceitful but not deceptive - time's tricks - time tricks. Refractive, geometric, optical overlay, a funhouse or circus or show with dancing girls - a little song and dance, extra extra, dog and pony, ringside attraction, why not - or an extremely and definitively quotidian progression as complex and as simple as walking across a room.

There is a sense of camaraderie across time and distance and process. There is process and idea clapped together, and the reverb off that clap. There is some epitome or there is no epitome. If the poet's art is to listen then there is sense to this otherworldy otherselfly transmission. There is a converse, a crossing into another space, a conversation and conversion, and there is this intimate ticking in six inside my head here and now. There is gratitude and there is exigency. There is no end to this; rather, there is a beginning, and here it is.

Dream distracts. Or is exactly the point. Over the years it has become much more so a writing-by-alarm: in 1994 - the year my 3:15s from the first to the eighteenth were stolen out from under a pool table at a Mekons show in Austin, Texas - I was awake at 3:15 almost every night all August. This writing-by-alarm is one out of a large - infinite? - bag of tricks. The self outside the self. To get ourselves to pay attention differently, unawares. It was Bernadette's idea. A kind of tracking device for a state between that world and this, a way of looking in on a self not your usual conscious self. Or conscious in a different way. A lull in the traffic, or a different kind of traffic.

The reflection of flame through glass looks like water on the wall. Water of light. You'd be correct, dear reader, in your suspicion that these texts were not edited from their original scrawlings. This project is not about the imposition of the waking (critical) (refined) mind on the 3:15 (raw) (critical) mind. Cannot be. It is about scratching a small transparent spot into the opaque surface of sleep, of dream, of our daily existence in that other nightly world, to see what is there. Merely what is there, merely to see.

—Jen Hofer April 20 - 28, 2001 3:15 A.M.
calle republica del salvador 31-52, mÈxico, d.f.

The 3:15 Experiment

August 1993-2000 3:15 A.M.

August 1

the lead deal
crack in the hurled world
a fast formed hybrid paper bird

(my half remembered turn in
some lost drunken exquisite corpse)

                                    —L.A.B.

from SOME LIKE IT HOT: why would a man want to
marry a man? Security.
northern exposure
cnn
how wordy i'm now not
dreamt i saw eliot
did you hit the right keys?
marriage
dreams
neurology tragedy in the sky
          tragedy in the sky
          a time for terror, or something like that
chuck berry
eliot greenspan
jackie joyner-kersee   jakeline joyner-kersee
this is a lousy bill - - -   charles rangel
a good political decision, a bad moral one
on clinton's signing the so-called welfare reform bill
(which _____ is against
          the heartland microbrewery (sucks)
          'william kuntsler has a book   (barnes & noble)
mobile mammography van - - Times Herald record
kate called for noah
suddenly you can remember all your dreams
you have sex. food and poetry as frequently as Patrick Henry and
John Paul Jones stood in a revolutionary room
both seem to have signed the declaration of independence

everybody calls you up all the time to ask you questions about
poetry (starring robert stack) (all women seem to have cancer)
Phil liked the untouchables and watched a lot of tv when he was in
the 7th grade. I don't know if i know anybody like that. Benjamin
Franklin is now in the movie. (played by charles laughton)
they seem to be at versailles. would finding out why certain letters
are on certain sides of the keyboard be as difficult as finding out
about my dreams? Am i a horrible person does rosemary think she
is a horrible person? today we are at a trattoria in somers. Phil
had penne in vodka sauce and i had a calzone. I have not yet
begun to fight. vinyl siding wash

—B.M.

late and dark I want to disappear into
the general you who you be me we and
this spiritual longing spiritual awakening spiritual
loneliness has occurred will occur because I know
time has stood still when I breathe a butterfly is born
200 years ago in the forest when I blink a thousand
dead leaves fall into your hand 50 years hence do you
believe me? Do you know what Buddha said time
is gone and love has taken its place eternal
in the stormy mass of matters eternal in pale skyness
eternal in the grand swell belly ache seriousness
of my deepening well I'm
trying to be full while you fly away
your memory fades do you remember the first
time you made love was it safe do you still
crave that nest are you home and when you
leave does your home come with you? take
me away flutter angel drag me thru stars
so like a galaxy like a constellation of burning
stars I tell you time does not exist and you
write poems for me on yesterday rocks I gaze
into tomorrow and see your voice a blanket of
songs trumpet and we march in one skin I told
you love was in your mouth I told you
you had wings they spread while I

2

grip the sidewalk trying to befriend spirits
helium balloon at the zoo why do the
monkeys and hyenas make you smile be sad for
me on the hot cement with my gripping feet be sad
that my knees are heavy and my belly soft and
potted why won't you be sad for me   If I
say fly you will never come back dear
candle light if I say fly you will forget my
eyes over your supper the nutrients like amnesia pills
filling you with pictures of words and things
resembling domestic animals we are not domestic
do you hear? We are meant to gnaw
on sound bites on fresh vision and
don't you like to masticate my little carnivore?
Chew the meat as you chew the meat your
memory fades what is love you ask. I
can't remember.

—D.D.

the ticking double, fractured, unframed
pulled apart to unravel
will get to it later or won't
small as if to say
there exists the possibility
of a different face though you've
grown accustomed to this one
under the sunken garden was another,
more detailed version
let's try harder starting now
black and white photos on wood
paneled walls and if the element
of forcing or doctoring exists
do you or don't you (do you not, sweets)
want to admit or spin
four jars full of dna, there
are people we do and don't know both
and the sound of a different am
(so we don't need to go other places).

the light had diminished synthetically
in reference pyramid us ok aka
primarily to being asked
which becomes more grainy
as it falls, separating.
clean river water under a
clean public works project about
to become the memory of sight

—J.H.

August 2

They say timing is a gift.
Like turquoise   Sky should
pull over & share the
duet
moving people A rock & roll
star.   like
picking 900 leaves
I
waver
hint
soak you like
a trouble shooter   small day
\in the middle of a page
Jazz   operations
skid kid trumpet
& the high sax.   Stay awake
let it work it's recognition

wail   wail

—D.D.

familiar, but late

if we are the labor

of poetry, then who is management

what laws govern it

show just cause you

have good luck with gum

or rather, congratulations

or the gum.

  Not cheating, but

late. Not Up at

the house by the lake

by the sky by

sutures by the

snares

we are jocelyn's

    elders

someone's kept

me in the

    dark on this.

                     —B.M.

being more more
important than (melodic
songs in memory or
stereo) noon having
tried — to try it having
being enough — making
moves so moving more — more
importantly — the sound on
the neck — of the finger
on the neck — i won't name-
drop —the president drove
by — so returning to the
original — thanks anyway — love, jen

                                        —J.H.

forming changes
funicular
  eye spans
pain — f
garlic heart

Don't Go
  Moon is
    rising

a prickly
  pear
flagellation
a ee i o u

first union

thelonious is looking
                over

                                        —L.A.B.

August 3

bending down to
the beating sound of train (artificial) as
accordions (stockinged feet) (flat bicycle
tires) of trains roiling towards
merely to start up again

was too hot to touch.

under the rafters
more rafters and a sense
of humor seared sullenly
into a blistering sky

a blistering blue (to follow) but pleasing to
eye and mystified (and then felt stupid) in
comparison with previous years (there's
no other word for it)

experiments in blindness charred
so ripe with black dust and then the sound
went dim out of not consideration
but sheer forgetfulness.

—J.H.

Let's pick up there we
          left off
I said globe and you
          picked a boy's journey
I said

I'd follow you to the ends of
   the earth
   you said   dangerous proposition

Air crisp hits this
    wine-tainted mind
    tipped slowly over
a longer day
I am saving gas by not
            driving my car
sometimes
            drinking as an excuse
Your body
voices in the room upstairs

She offers fresh bread
            and sauteed
mushrooms because
food is life and if there is
nothing to say   well then

So anxious to be out of
            my clothes   as
house ghosts witness my
            strip tease
sometimes it's cats
            catch me off guard
I'm working again
making a go

You said maybe this isn't
    what you are supposed
    to be doing
I said   I am built for speed

You ask
            How can I make it   all
            up to you   I want
                    to take you somewhere
Tell me everything that is
            in your heart
starting with last night

I iced my swollen face

this morning so I could
   exist outside   but
spent most of the day swallowing
my words   I couldn't *do* anything
   until I heard your voice
Knew that we could go on   see
a future didn't exist until I
knew we could understand
            each other again if
only on 2 sides of
         a phone line

You say
   I woke up
   I felt bad
And sound it
Nothing of this matters
when I am this tired
            no more wine
bartender
I need to be untied
            it jumps inside
this person
            trying to listen
ears cracked   heaven
   gestures
   Anyone home?

   Let's not fight
   subliminal
hand painted   desire
hopscotch   bourbon   seminary
            tasteless   subtle
barbaric   I am
running out of places to go.

                              —D.D.

No more due to this

and due to that —

   if we're that

then let us have   it

right away . above the gray

city let's exchange possible

vacation

this man asked for

chief of staff but was

too numb by standards

of common following

oh very fucking clever

get a child to sell

really there's no reason

too vile

—B.M.

vervaine
virtu

virtual
  real
   tight
power surge
  sore

the verse police
aren't around

pomegranate
falcon
cris de corps
  sprocket
cheer trish
content of dream
more girlic
not felt sirrah
a complete sentence — ah
not as much
thinking about writing
but yet writing
anyway — wild writing
much generation
  of separation
degrees of messy writing
Formal meadows
Oxymoronic sashes
small pages herald
dry oh it's "just us"
a drawing
wha — wanting to
conceal my weapon
I might not
have, I spoke a
net, delayed,
Then said it loud —
surprising upheld

city in the clouds,
apart from the
world yet connected
cath catylystically
enough
    Tasting late
Formal meadows
Tasting late

swa
suede you guess
        what
little select &
    free dishes

—L.A.B.

August 4

the upstairs was gone but expansion
the walls widened & more space
on all light sides. could suggest
trumpets or dunce caps, even
legal documents in unintelligible
full sentences. what other kinds
of sentences are there? cacophonic
influence of dust, invasive nudity,
apprehension & global warming.
windows open for punctuation & slowly
we learned that the body has parts.
city siren's illogic interrupted
bluster's ballast in whimsy of frenzied
gardeners: not from this neighborhood
nohow, not at the museum but near
it, where the parking's free.

—J.H.

oh, right — I forgot about other countries

that have similar mechanisms; I mean

for a second without performing

I almost leaped. No looking.

But now light forwards of everything.

Who will complain? my love or

nicer odd balls?

Idle hours make fortunate hands —

bees mingle where tie-rods dim.

These are prophecies of my

youth. And so good night.

—B.M.

(tale of the Future Muse)

    In the dark
precious mosquito light
that glowed perched none
other than the itch
to tell.   A
joyous occasion this
when triggered fell

plop thud like an

iceberg.   No bevy
or slough

                made much mess
but what a quality
very round like shoulders
like certain shoulders I've
seen in memory. Yes,
womanly shoulders, what
curvature.
                But, when
asked, I politely
declined.
                Was I thinking
of a better offer? This was
the good chip knocked
off

"You better tell me what's
going on!" I attempted
    But still were
those northern lights.

Still wasn't an answer
or question. Still was
    laid to rest. Was
the worst over or yet to
    come? Is it fair to
ask the future muses
    such things?   why

not if we're trapped here
of our own accord. No
help from
                Apollo   or Zeus.

    The muse winced as
we brought her in,
supported under the arms and
    leaning on my shoulder.

So, there we were.

"It's all the same
moment," laughed future

muse, smiling at
the irony.
"It's all the same
moment." It was my
turn to wince. I did

not enjoy puzzles

and ending was
always so painfully
difficult. But, then
again, I guess
she'd already done
it for me. She
bit my ankle

"You still don't see."

—D.D.

Awake in Boulder
Reading about
Awake in Spain
my parents' anniversary now
Bought a Ganesh today &
incense. Had dinner with
Judy, Steven, Peter L. Wilson,
Nick Amster, Rani Singh,
Steve Myles, Judy & Steven
are at Judy's tonight.
I've eaten so much today—
Juaninta's & Sushi the
night before. Two bad

movies — *Poetic Justice* &
Robin Hood: Men in Tights.
Tomorrow I'll fly across 2
time zones to NYC where I
hope it's still not the heat wave
and the water is full of
bacteria. No one. I am
writing with Danika now
& Myshel & Jenn

(illustration of time zones)

tomorrow I will move to
position/zone B & K then in
a week or two (?) Jenn will go to SF
zone 0
pretty graphs
I remember celebrity
New Year's Eve with
champagne on a plane
flying West to SF,
landing & having enough
time for Julie to drive me
to a party in time for
their mid-night—
an Indian fete.
   What happens at 3:15?
It's interesting to have an
event to look forward to
in what's usually
the secret middle of the
night in
"August is the secret month."

   It's cold here &
I have 2 blankets. I
hear a raccoon!
I will now read some more Frank O. bio &
sleep once more under
the fluorescent stars

we saw revolving
stoned on Klezmeow
music.

—L.A.B.

August 5

To Scale

Under a full sky
traffic was very light and
the shadows flickered fetchingly.

There we go ripping the newspaper
so carefully lining the bottom
of our cage and there we go
surefire way to get us in a state

Commerce hums with not needing less, (not needing us)
lopsided and so more lovable
down and down the street
"not too much goin' on upstairs," commented
the meter maid, whose uniform was
pleasantly too tight.
"I can hardly stand myself."
the cherry pits, rose thorns and
chicken feet amassed beside us
as the even work-a-day
            evening wore on

the reprise began and began again
there was a special spot for contest submissions
as for the context, it kept swelling and
                swelling until we — we felt that
truly we would burst with the pizzaz of
    our little secret

—J.H.

working in paris, how many

articles can you find? gli viali

Romani sono molto multi

because, as if, so
        that —

and nothing nothing nothing nothing

translated
and nothing breaks

—B.M.

Lightning Storm

Midnight lights the expanse
        of horizon
slowly the grumble grows   I
was dreaming of four separate
men each I love
            with different breath and
                    reason
        they are   haphazard
Bright spark beyond clouds
        silhouettes the gray or
streaks of long electricity punch
        the earth
My men are boys
weak and strong
They occupy too much of my mind
and alone time
I tire of waiting   a
crowd at the Impressionist
        exhibit
                spontaneous strokes

                    simple life
a flash of moment
makes love   bolt
Never strikes the same note twice
my men are passing fancies
              go   go   storm I
want to sleep   the
cat in window trains his
              eyes
on the storm   say
the strike is beautiful
              from a distance   but
the noise keeps us awake
I expect I will have
              none of them
                        in the end
pass time
              I suspect beautiful mess
it never stops here   everything always
goes and goes   father-in-law
              said   looking out towards
              the sound   goes and goes
Ah, the rain, it is here.

                                        —D.D.

So sleepy behind the flowers
at Bernadette's. She's in the
shower - one clock says 3:17
but it's probably fast. My parents
were married yesterday 31 yrs
ago. Today S. & I were talking about
how marriage is a strange concept —
it seems so outwardly defined —
hard to "be different" & hard
not to be.
    Thursday, my second chapbook
a **muse**me was published

by Boog Lit. I just opened
the new selected Robert D. &
saw "For a Muse A Meant"
for the first time.
   What? A Spice level.
Talking loudly in the heatly
Hope the cats are still
not in the heat that is
not summer. "I remember
white spots on fingernails"
Knock yourself out why
don't you.
Large oil painting & teddy
bears. Dissatisfied cramp-
ing. Sunfrog & Lisa are
having a baby. Flowers
have a kiss-in. Is "it"
pleasure? Don't blame me.
Cosmopolitan. Lolita.
oil cosmic mopsmoll tan
not comma. Wilting wit
kin to my perfidy. What.
The beach bell trunk sting
chains it back crab.
Addressing you directly.
O famous with. O
spurious play. Drooping
sustaining, lean & fragen.
unsatisfactory closure.
Remember the Renga:
O vowels are you there
inherent critique on form
homophically
lost or toasted. Living
somewhere else. A garden
on top of the cave-house.

_____

How smooth the page on
which my skin or hand rests while
Bernadette still writes

overlay of in-
fluence awaits our
unsteady gait
I would like that
photon graphed upside
your head so as to
press on or apply pressure
to your vital organs.
Peels Sleep
Sleep O to Peels
¡Peels O to Sleep!
Yawning gnawing
          group portrait quit up
ticking or else sour
Sleep! Morpheas
James Dean joined
Frank O'Hara for a drink.

O for a rof o

O for a roof
O for a Fool
O for a Foot
O for a fact
O for a f-note

                               —L.A.B.

August 6

four—for

can't—

can't—

for
some sense
more space
between
slow

—J.H.

damn i wish phil

would have a better birthday

also a room where

my nakedness was

discouraged.

or my italian

sketches might all at once

follow the path of sky

painted above weehawken like

pretzels.

no one circled

the buses; soon

though we'll be

naked.

—B.M.

smoke hangs in air around city
even in dreams I make phone
calls to eastern Europe 15 mangosteens
chase me down because what?
I was remembered   *sola*
big pans and once, rows of people
walk home it's the
we *arrive* trepidation
I draw I suppose
Isn't this ego in dose
of Napoleon to carry
a son echoes through
the traffic blur   ancient
and lonely

It was just after the earthquake
when the 2nd and 3rd fires started.
Welcome to Bosnia, Jen and I joked,
another day in the life in Mostar.
Perhaps the earthquake set off a
land mine or it spontaneously combusted
in the heat. We cringe and laugh nervously.
Vasvija brings a bowl of fresh
watermelon to counteract the heat and
we watch the fires burn like its
our entertainment for the evening
          A few blocks away
the remnants of a shelled building

recovery is slower in Bosnia. Don't
have the economy for it. *This*, Jen
says, *is some fucked up shit.*

—D.D.

    providential
    providence
    ecnedivorp

The black cattens are
sucking on each other's
necks on the purple
bath rug. I think Bim is
doing it to Bom.
Orally teething on my pen
she is now biting to find
out what's going down.
S. fell asleep & then got
hard, his soft skin.
M. is making me nervous
slightly, pulling head trips.
The twins are sleepily
purple, side by side, now
coming to lay one of their
heads upon the
smooth page
smearing the ink—
   with spittle moist throat
fur, gnawing the pen,
biting my thumb.
Cat spit—what I
allergic to & irresistibly
rubbing late night.
A creaking warm flour board,
no more aspirin.
Writing in the kitchen
the bathroom—

cat leaping up impossibly.
Floweredy patterns, forms
to fill out. Interruptions
abound. Even at this late
hour. Lipstick impudence.
Older pills of glockenspiel
lettuce. A shadowy umbra
umbrella cinderella.
Allowed to be silly or
expected to not make
a whole lot of sense.
Say something "deep."
Providence me with
a job & a dictum
to live by. Or not.
paisley behind closed lids or
more ring-like white
gathering speed as his thumbs
pressed outwards.
Appearing muse like in the
air, a giant moth was
there for us all to see.
She touched it & it flew
for us.
There is a Zone
whose even Years
No solstice interrupt.
O — my bone was stolen—
did I tell you — the
wrestling kitten elk thigh
jointed censure
relaxed mexico
pr free castle is
I've land rest
fog mushroom farm
repeat input
variation
clutter
muff.

       —L.A.B.

August 7

fog and flame, scuff
and skin unwound, hunger
leaden like a new season.
the harpsichord of rivalry
sings flat and furious, a dim
fog with obtuse perimeter
silent eventually.

sleep is a beeless silent honey.
a closed watery throat.
shoeless dancing on asphalt
and ragged, sore but unscathed.

the bombs continue to punctuate
elsewhere. our neighborhoods
believed safe inhabited, like some
overture whose music surely follows.
a bellows wheezes in and out
anemic but functioning, fanning
what fire there is after
months of rain and rip.

—J.H.

If my head were any thicker
    I'd be an ocean
I am under water fluent in
my dream tongue
prone to fantasy
fantastic in proportion
proposing an end to all this
        terrific brain chaos
my vocabulary is slipping my
verbs have become weak

word muscle blowout I've
popped a nerve
jacked up on this quarrelsome ride
sleep, rest, dream   solitude
There are 100's of ways to kiss the sky
There are 100's of ways to divert
your heart

It is the season for so many things

passes by. winks. dives.   it's
coming I know it's coming   I'm
spending all my summer days
worried about winter
wound up in gut socks
pounced on by laughing gods
ho-ho-he-ho

Tell me the story about the theater again
How you went there with your father and everyone
made you feel so empty and lonely inside
It was sensual and gothic
It lacked a mother
You need feminine influence you need an
angel on your shoulder
Pool our resources and what do we get?
2 pairs of hands
a lake of tears the voice of a sage
the heart of a child

Too many pages
Too many letters   too may breaths held
hold on   my life

curtain call

—D.D.

hey hey   how many kids
did you kill today
the light at the end is the black and white dog
sweltering work, bye see ya,
jean giorno, b.h. friedman the art critic
the strawman, the striped towel!
the norton anthology of modern poetry
men sometimes speak louder than women
i saw that god was dead on t.v.
it's yom kippur
maybe it's both neurological and true.

—B.M.

Kittens knock over water
and the breeze is fighting for
me to stay awake.
"I do this, I do
that." Cut backs:
go away. I sing
and I am happy.
The kittens step
on the clock
& jazz comes on.
Today many things
happened including
talking to Rosemary
C. about coming in
Wednesday at 10 for
an interview I
presume. The
Cordettes wrestle
ousted from my
bed. Coltrane was
here, now someone
else. Sang a
cat version of "Come
Again" tonight.

The magic of the voice.
A 600 acre ranch
overlooking the Pacific
Ocean. Wait til I
tell the folks!
False Prophets dropped
their name and provide
no replacement.
In the dark of the night,
THE HAIR RULES.
I didn't do my NEA
_____? today. Resolve
no more all nighters—
can I still work.
All nighters only
for poetry.
In my mind
Frank O. writes
another I do this
I do that poem
as I don't even smoke
the journal entry.
The LISA power is
strong tonight—
She's a great artist.
Blonde tough light
on motion sounding
dark too. Work it
Girl
Poet.

Leonine Brown pads
summerly up to

A Leonine Browed
animal pads summerly
up to Carnal Knowledge

Beverly Dahlen
B

Revelry Dahlia
Revery
Reverdy
She said now that
or even though we're
the best of friends,
I won't tell you
what I'm going to
do yet.

—L.A.B.

August 8

dear pamplemousse:

this is the undreamt record of the places i haven't been.
the howling cat named dracula. maul equals language.
here's the full sentence you asked for. when did furniture
become conservative? with a cloudy background and two clocks—
what else?—ticking without intention of music in a mart
world where no sale is final.

—J.H.

about cheating or the clocks wrong . . .

who cares why we say things

thinks is a harm . things make

fucking us like a walk in the park.

i have it on file.

means of us — fair-haired, billowing.

It is at least sight my

afro-pick, washed as yet

still ever green

over grown night , calyx and

capsule ever now, asleep

and staring into the green stars .

we wake to this, sweating .

we see again all life rising to meet us

as though we were silent,

as though we didn't know.

—B.M.

Not sure what time it is. Watch woke me up at 3:15 but I
went back to sleep w/it in my hand. Woke up to this vision of men
making deals. Men making deals and giving them long strange
names
like Half Pipe Moral Hangover W/ a Twist. I had
another dream earlier and I was very sad in it but I don't
remember why. Did someone die? In the end I was hugging
this young guy — old friend of mine and everyone was staring.
We had just gotten out of a movie theater so I used that as an
excuse. Sad movie.

Can't think can't turn left turn right blood in piles like ponds a
small river a white shirt soaked in it a car alarm an ear on the
floor shut that damn alarm off. A burglar in our neighborhood?
Might he steal the dirty laundry in the back of my car?

Would we be w/out

                       a psychotic man

clothes naked.
with a gasoline can a robbery a man talking and sounding like an
automatic voice a robotic voice a communication a mix-up Joe,
big Joe w/a gun A man w/ a beard. Mr. Brown (the director) is
dead Mr. Blue is dead (a minor character). Mr. Orange lies
bleeding in a pool of his own blood. The traitor, not a traitor to
cops, a traitor to the robbers. An undercover job. He reminds
me of an old friend from Berkeley who now lives in Jersey &
owns 3 coffee shops. He had a great singing voice. Well

this cop reminded me of him. Mr. Pink the guy who had a beard.
He's nervous says fuck too much but then again they all do. This
guy doesn't get shot by his own men — but outside off camera the
cops get him. You hear yells bullets (yes shots) and screams—
good effect. Mr. Blonde thank god was shot by Mr. Orange that
guy he was so psychotic. He cut off the kidnapped cop's ear &
was going to set him on fire, until Mr. Orange shot him. He
blew it in the first place by going on a shooting spree during the
heist because some employee tripped the alarm. Mr. White I
kinda liked, the most moral of the robbers you might say.
Tried to protect Mr. Orange because he didn't think he was a
traitor & got shot for that by fast talking Eddie, Joe's son. Mr.
White would only shoot cops, no "normal" people. Joe, big fat
Joe, and Eddie are in charge. Joe shoots Orange White shoots
Joe & Eddie shoots White. Wait, Eddie goes down too — who
shoots Eddie?
                   It's like a Shakespeare play D said. Yeah, like
Hamlet, everybody dies. We shared w/ Gary a pound of jelly
beans surprised I didn't get sick w/beer and my medication,
amoxicillan, for my emergency root canal. Yeah, that's how I
started my day. An hour in the dentist's chair my tooth is dead
and gone dead dead dead as a door knob the roots
have shriveled up and it's dead dead dead gone. Day started
w/ death and violence & ended the same way. It's a
wonder I'm not having nightmares well maybe I am I still
haven't figured out why I was crying.

                             —D.D.

"Es macht kein Unterschied."
Harry in the air.
A diagram of muses,
days, 7 of us (one
secret) Steven
observes our drunken
neighbors how they can
only listen to taped music
when a live one shows up
they don't want to hear it
R-O-Y-G-B-I-V
diagrams of time
machines, plant houses,
wet lands sewer systems
"Affair" need S. singing
anger at having to
take charge, be
responsible.
Money in the monkey.
Singing to the baby.
Cause we don't like their
social animals.
Bee stung lips & eye
lids heavy with Peter
Rabbit all night up
late gender robbing.
Thinking you're in the
middle ground is
essential to being able
to write high theory.
Too much aspiration=
Writer's block BIG
TIME.
Graffitti Partch
method. It's
3:15 & "I'm
hungry & broke. I wish
I were dead."
This product was
made of fine Austra

Lian brandy -------
Airshow danger. Walking
naked by the windows
whispering between my
fiance & my what?
Live evil
Love evol
Love vole
  evolve y'all
mange merger
Wet without having to
go. Reading everything
backwards. Sustain &
believe — something prevails,
pressed and dried flowers
to seek out my son.
Myson & what about
my daughter. Better to
have an older daughter,
or an evil empire
threatens to pounce
in my clouded brain.
udder nonsense
bubba incense
truculent pearls that
were his eyes suet
solo. Tuesday mojo.
They're all wasted, showing
not telling. Nickel
Eastwood. Marriage
as a cover. Retro
Aether red Lion
I want to see my old
bedroom of when
I was 0-10
1955-1965 Almost
to the month S. Says.
Really to the month.
Feb 55-Mar 55
How long do babies stay in

the hospital
I remember her bringing us
malt. She put it on
the Dodo. What's
that? *Dodo?*
Pacifier. She did a wonderful job.
The tit. The
codliver oil.
A kind of tonic.
a vitamin B supplement.

—L.A.B.

August 9

Are we this trainable
        some
        out
from our cages you can not
 get any closer even if you
        were skin
running around   trying to be someone
        discover now
          this
        body a raft
moving   leader a
       stop
-ing   to be just that
& nothing more
        self
        (age)
        done

—D.D.

one was about night,

one was all Greece

each in the small cell

abiding, stretched upon a pallet

    bed

    this is it, now

    all you ever have

                     —B.M.

a memory of memory
or slips out (labor through eyelets,
teeth, thread) thank you between
breaths

like most things, they started small

a nation of tardy resources
slipknots unsilking

sabotage continual
over a period filling the sky motor-like

you can tell a lot from
the cracks. from the ground.
to leave a thing for later

the sound faded, but not really

                    —J.H.

Morning & Night of
Thunder Rain & then it
came to pass
that the long gold hair
came out of the grave
& grew like golden
grass
The forces & powers
of lightning disrupting
our peaceful stay (?) is
the late-night horrors —
imbalance—necessary for
growth & change— but
nightmarish for
Libras— A Libran nag—
balance it out! Aquarian
S. is pouring forth his
generous intimacies
somatic. Just enjoy (?)
instead of check &
balance. Things
must tilt the balance
in order to change-a
constant tuning (?)
Bodily painful manifestations
of dissatisfaction &
waiting to argue.
People have different needs.
—Sometimes it's not fair.
The paperwork. I've
got it. hysterics
(a disease of the attention)
How can it be resolved.
In time. In place.
Chaotic/Dark he solves
revolves with time.
Bad habits intrench get
stuck, need to be interrogated.
Mind advisor, another point
of view. Life is not a

mystery novel or shld not
be a psycho-drama.
Glossy mad wounded child.
of the universe.
At peace with certain
aspects of yourself. I
need not to be in this
fighting environment.
Don't drive me out of my
own skull space home
please.
Alice in chaos. (?) The
nightmare realm *can*
look forward to having
breakfast.
Leonine, at night I
roar.

_____

A Leonine Browed
Pet pads summerly toward
Carla Knowledge

                        up to

a Leonine Browed
—— ——— pads summerly up
                        summarily

up (strike through)
to Carla Knowledge

A Leonine Browed
_____pads summarily up
to Carla Knowledge
A Leonine Browed
verb tense pads summerly up
to Carla Knowledge

A Leoinine Browed
method pads summerly up

to Carla Knowledge
  Carnal?

Not 3:15

The Ballad of the Blonde Hair
—
Humidly bored
What would happen if
they picked where
they grew?

———

Stein O Rama
gertrude
  chic
  Ochishii

                              —L.A.B.

August 10

enola gay smithsonian
suicide kevorkian everything is so difficult
to understand i never could write and i can't seem
to write now — some people never seem to want to write
at all— maybe i should try something else ; i always confuse
myself with other people; somebody says to somebody: how
much were you earning before you struck it rich (with your
movie)? somebody answered, $18,000. somebody laughed (and
you were kissing somebody's ass as well, somebody said) /.
Nobody seems to think your an interesting writer either.
who can i talk to? whom believe? engineer. joe ceravolo,
george berlant, all the students at the stevens institute.
kool-aid, guyana? escape fom los angeles, john sayles.
feeling bad is good - that's what many people believe.

to refine one's attitude to telling the truth - i know everything
by heart -what does broad daylight mean? pleine soleil -
purple noon, but can i hold down a regular job

—B.M.

sometimes it's easier just not to
          start   then the expec-
tation of self dissolves
into inner eye
                    I watch
now others pass me by
          and I'm still in love
all this time
          then I'm in pain it
          jolts me back to that
first year when I had time

energy only to letter a day
for you keep none for
myself   two dogs on a hunting
                    trip
one drowns the other   hibernates
but together both learn the
          power of dream

On a more positive note
we have been reincarnated
          into something
but too baby to understand
          what
inner eye stings
          imagine
                    manatee
performed loquacion:

          kiss

when everyone else is
coupling like kindling
we grow distant
into each other
she said
   there was in my dream
   an angel at the door
   he gave me a dollar
   I thanked him he
   flew to the moon
I said
   I like the part about the angel

He said
   I opened the water
   and there was a ship
but he was unable to
   share this with us
quiet intellectual   who
will inevitably be lost at
   sea

clever girl who will
never get her piano lessons
life teaching at YMCA
center in housing project
jokes about horse-hair
weaves a girl about
to throw a metal chair
   friend stops her
little girl who
whispers in my ear

   My sister lost her baby
or
   My mom's boyfriend treats
   her nice he gave her $200

         —D.D.

dear yellow—

still not still. an hour
can be troubled, flickers,
anemic. silver not
silver. don't listen.
later sugar in collected
corners. to mimic dust,
sight, ligature. wasn't
the   he asked so
slow down commonly.
solo feature, fixit tune.

—J.H.

Dream:
Naropa President offers Rani Singh a job at the Los Angeles
Campus
    of Naropa. He's the author of the faery book. I tell him I love
    the water nixie as I finish my pile of lambchops in the fancy
NYC
    restaurant-club. Jennifer/Janie comes in.
    Also I eat monarch butterflies in a sweet slightly chrystalized
cream
    sauce out of a jar.

—L.A.B.

August 11

slipped and skidded into a heartfelt
haircut where the beer is darker
and your jaunty doorstep trips me
every time. the number of steps
in the procedure is one hundred

sixty, the number of swallows trapped
in the stucco called past history is
ninety-nine, a cusp being an edge
or pressure to fall from. cusped,
held instantly. preserved, we haunt
in categories. just in case. bygones.
unforgettable. negotiations having undone
us to this small stature, now in need
of some respirator, some lovelorn
machination to aid in the shift
of position, the rearrangement of limb
and harness, map and continent.

—J.H.

Day angels that remind you
        Laughter
           songs that make you forget
like today
soft sun
park not in ruin
life in array

Eigner says each moment is a whole
life in life taken   we are
lincoln logs   cats in glass houses
and I want to say groovy
there's much to do but taken 3 at
        a time tasks commence
No more strange tigers
no more breathing turtles
just pages and pages turn turn turn
it's been summer a long time
        been wanting to tell you of
                this
me down on earth
      why you came
      to save a life and now

you are free   my lightness is
your lightness my high-ness is your
            high-ness
            Dig deep bones always
smell-
            ing salt   earth   day
there is so much time now
glass beads eventually
            sand
                        I bring you more heart
you give good mind
            I pay attention
this thick air
waves of it   no silence
but to hear   it all over
again   each day
            jab   note   wake
summertime and the living are alive

Go & do   go & do
            like that
it can be   harder but why?
            das kind war
            wen das kind, das kind war
                        You knew what you
            were doing all along
coyote angel
                        baby
doo-wah   doo-wah
            curtain call
            the angel curious came
& there was much celebrating
& no overnight hospitalizations
only mexican jumping beans
Sylvester the cat
            and *licht, mier licht*

                                    —D.D.

Exclamation of
Floating bear milk
Soppishly try for surrealism
as chain letters mend
my headache still here.
Cherry cola in the
car still driving along
with out us towards
the south. Reading this
over ground me
temporarily to a halt.
Today's idea: the
Betty Feezor show.
Do something with the tapes.
Short kittenbreak. Bom
won't let me wrote!
going crazy! I
'm going to derange yr.
senses & se how you
like that!
My other hand is now
providing a decoy pen
so I can use
this one! What
a trial!
Then off the lights

—L.A.B.

vintage seltzer water
s. pellegrino water
lemon lime rebound rortified quencher
almaden mountain burgundy
white rose spring water
nytimes week in review august 11, 1996
nytimes unfurnished manhattan apts3,4 and 5 rooms
bks by frida khalo, and merrill gilfillan
catalog - moyer bell

latin grammar
anthology an ear to the ground
pansy - pensee

—B.M.

August 12

pair bonding
abdominal icicles jim jones I'm watching guyana
tragedy nothing about flight 800 the rasberry
soda is sweet hollywood ideology james reston father
divine star quality nuclear holocaust hippie communal
and civil rights eye care office
powell to the people - - ny daily news

—B.M.

it's too late
at this early
hour to be properly
considered as morning
as cloud
swinging lonely
and inveterate in
the absence of sky

—J.H.

I was writing down
all of it, conversation
and sound
voice defensive   this
is my artistic self

I'm not apologizing
it's just the way it is with me
I've fallen into my chaos and
can't get up

we were talking just before
midnight I wanted to clear
the air   he said
I don't think I'm asking you
to say anything

I am a great observer of my emotions
they remind me over and over again
that I am human
           it's
wait and see mode
six of one half a dozen of the other
you get older and you kick yourself
but I don't look back much
I learn as I go
stay where I am

All this writing business
restless cats
DREAM:
woman kisses me bitterly
It's not the taste I expect
was looking for a little softness
ex-student beaming romantically
or attempting to be
involved with me I say
you are half my age
woman or man — you are too
young (at 16) for me
she was adamant
infatuated

you have to dance around heavy
concepts because words are inadequate
to explain some things

obsessed
women lovers who only meet
me in dreams
where are you soft lips
your fleshy flesh
I have been here all
along
basically you're damned

> *don't spit into the wind*
> *enough of this silliness*
> *just get your work done so we can go to*
> *Vancouver*

my dynamic aches
          pendulums at the
bottom of my will
Oh God   I've become
a ritual
          and now
you won't talk to me
line please:

> *yeah, I knew her*
> *she's a very interesting woman*
> *but she just didn't*
> *have enough time*
> *her creative juices were always flowing*
> *and not over me*

You may have just lost
the best thing that
ever happened to you
I know   I know

—D.D.

    Rebel sleep the
night of Orlando &
the Persoid meteor shower
provided quiet.
A blood red blood is
bleeding. 3 lovely beings all
sprawled out of their
senses. Perpetual
headache, waking
or sleeping, a paw closes
the book. What was the
Closerie de Lilas?
A closet of lilies?
Barbara Guest guessed
O'Hara didn't follow
until sailor suit one
there finished the job—
Nelly's swollen eye. Nipples at Dusk!
I respective itch.
Occasional poetr.
Birthday poems all
around! Good one may take
years to prepare. Motivated
by wanting transport to
unjealous states of motion.
a dinner we all enjoyed
had gotten along with
people better. O sky.
Schuyler beautiful
new collected works.
Finished orange chipping.
Phraseology out of fat or
should I say plump
plectral comets
masquerading as female
beings. Knowing that androgynous
person is important.
Lush blue black points.
Kissing like eating
under meats or

fruits. A dark lion.
A comfortable friar.
A compact fountain.
Gender specific wigs.
Rubbing gender at
once, all ways.
Brave new physics,
not so new after it
exposed how old Orlando
was, in leather with a
daughter. Cranach
red haired umbrage
varnished
darker cool. What
could it be like to have
a black velvet fur face?
   Nails trimmed & new
brown or auburn ruff,
my little love, still a
girl.

—L.A.B.

August 13

charming hostess

is perfect
my most
seven minutes
abbreviated
saturation six
minutes to hesitate
actually in millimeters
is feeling tactile
as opposed to

once again

would absolute be in
the absence of a behavior
appropriate sentence
or appropriation
toward seeming effortful
too extreme so will suffice coffee

this time with both hands
and an adequate understanding
undermined in low-rise state
capitol if we could pause
could slip could double remember
last year how inflected how
asphalt kicks in with
lines around the eyes and someone
to talk to

—J.H.

almost full moon over Croatia

you are looking out onto an
orange ocean there are loved
ones in disguise of seahorses
they blink in dreams and bring
you fresh cabbages they storm
several castles and call it a day
you are writing a letter to
your mother who lives in a
pigeon hole you may feed her
nibbles of corn in the courtyard
on a good day you have
forgotten that your life
is a handful of moments and that
one day you will join your
family tree in the great rotation

you look this up in a dictionary
and it says: begin here
you order a plate of buttons
and sew them to your sleeve the one
made from a flag that waved
from the chimney signaling your birth
you are dreaming again you wake
to find all your comforts
stolen you start over under
an alias and ask to be relocated
to the seaside
you pick mushrooms and basil
you write a book you
staple all your spare minutes inside.

—D.D.

Nova on no avon
Nova O No avon
Sumerian tree goddess blocking the view of she
golden throws serve soft
the way the best whines of my generator
were off in a flash
blew the fuse sitting in my lap
disappointment injury
inquiring you know what wants you to know
reverse sisters
programs relax into get going whats up

Vine form
        torch your
guard in
        hell broad
fever few
        chain link
kiln natch
        room morrison

moor rune
        creature dream
        come back unstolen
fast
to fat minus s
Friday the 13th
thirteenth
cooper sky
symmetry unfold in her baby
hair
O Kelly O
wool folks wiles

                        —L.A.B.

marion barry rikck barry marion farrier wendell berry
james carville al franken robert francis kurt russel bertrand
russell george bernard shaw saudi arabia max warsh marier warch
sophie warsh jackie shumanski vi. warshawski mel torme robert
altman russell day philip good lee ann brown harry truman barry
farber idt ron kuby mariah scoon jackson maclow andrew levy
andrew stumpf bernard goetz theodore mayer marie stumpf mayer
gerard rizza helen decker gary gullo eddie blenz eddie pepitone
jennifer jason leigh mirandaa richardson

                        —B.M.

August 14

Thelonious
       Alone
Ah poetry
  don't leave me now
  clutching at your diaphanous
    filmy gown
      crazy with
        insecure loneliness
    wading into the night alone
Monk
Alone in
San Francisco

running out into the street

_____

reading at the Waldrops
In England Now That Spring

  Steve MacCaffrey &
  bp Nichol

AYA 1979

_____

Sept_____
Oct_____
Nov_____
Dec_____

Silent Teachers
Remembered Sequel

(sketch)

Hannah Weiner

───

Reading
The Homosexual
in Society

Celadon
cobalt
Definitions

<u>Poetry</u>

a condensed form
of food & time

<u>Voice</u>
my speech
babe

run the
CoLabs throughout the
books
Colab 1: Thought
CoLab 2:

<u>Brain</u>
A rain in B
<u>Boat</u>
Toy bot,
a ted debt

<u>Solitude</u>
Sun in a squee-
          gee

<u>Modesty</u>
the ruined package

<u>Discourse</u>

talking fancy
without much too
drink

———

Looked at Magritte
poems, Wieners
Chinoiserie

felt craxy & sad

Wadlrop versus
Waldrop

Awake in another
               place
Drawing a schedule
of our writing
7 women
7 days/week
muses etc.

(circular sketch)

Dream: I kiss
Robert Kelly & thank
him for the poem only
to find out his name's
Tina Darraugh-
She is ecstatic
that I kissed her &
lifts me high—
No more of this silliness!
Tabitha! Mudra
armband. Ganesh
or Lakshmi.
40 situp crunches.
Hurt eye, a pungent smell.
Insecurity of love.
Bases covered or not.

A Performance Transform.

For every daffodil you
find, pluck it & replace
it with its dictionary
definition.
  I want to be
    adored now.

Print this in red on
cream paper & release
the whole thing into a lake.

in a dream begininng with the thought of skirts

Amazed at my inattention
        She had a hard day.
With a football player
        Who just started reading books.
Cued in cobalt eyes nested in a
        Variety of expensive shops
    She keeps going under, not wanting
The ideals to lavenderunder or
  Slip into inaccesible caverns
        of eyeless spider fishnet stockings

O'hara Mars in the paper
Litter lit. til re tiller
Take it easy give yourself
  Focus soon or all
Wash face & Hope
everything's been

sit
yet another break
it tossed
for the best
seeming very minimal
got to do
something big
from
here

                —L.A.B.

fallible purity
directional indications, motion symbol
hungry or nourishing
we wanted for the light to change
to indicate motion

illness as an indicator of physical
fallibility, the triumph of the animal
time's narrowing bestiary

waning more quickly to a flown point
swallowed like a flame or an argument
left behind in the cops' quick sweep of the neighborhood
unmarked, unobtruding, noticeable
waiting for the appropriately indicated moment

                —J.H.

this is the republican national convention period
tttttt
juon mccain gillian mccain legs diamond the mcneil
lehrer report william burroughs teri polo calvin
klein ruth anne miller
allen rothenberg allen ginsberg jerome rothenberg
my //   ralph ginsberg
test   solveig westerfield

```
               sylvia sleigh exercise this is not my country
               touch your elbow
     your      wake up little suzie
               diane powers they grind their corn
     your
     your      name is !!!        bernadette whatever
```

—B.M.

Low rider

still up at this hour
              after all these years
let me explain
   caught listening with glass
      against a wall

pain is an excuse and an excuser
I take my time now because no
one will take it for me
I carve space out   bring
   it out
      prime selection
      modern appetite

If it's not a pleasure
If it fails to surprise
If it doesn't come back
If it can't fit in this box
If it has no weight

tired of her own game
passing the ball
not afraid to let go
not afraid to go under
not afraid of proximity
   shooting star
   chalk outline

        fetal position
the nights between
        adding up and going nowhere
                no fear
monotony what kills us
    our own mind
    dancing circles
    into the light

pain is   monotony
    mutiny
            her own bodied
                    betrayal
all the best hiding places gone
all the obvious ones
                    too far
distance becomes time
    measured by   language
you said you'd be here
and everything already invented
        just improving itself
            for   resale

Ambition
creation
backbone

                        —D.D.

August 15

something about substance or
how when you look at an object
it's to evaluate its solidity
in the aura analogy
we make friends
full moon over *Muzeum*
the uncomfortable-ness of a pub seat
glances
to look out
somewhere between apathy and
            disapproval
there I go again

the shape and working of boxes of foreign food
shopping carts
how easily red wine goes down
a bed on the floor
a floor for a bed
the difference between Henry
Miller in Paris and a photograph
2nd hand war stories
describing the color of water
feeding addictions
the time it takes for my thoughts
            to get to you
you and you and you
the air underground
the view of a gathering crowd from above
after earlier being one of the crowd
blinded clockmakers
forgetting to read a poem
the color magenta we travelers
            have in common
the apology after a touch
acting like tourists
happily acting like tourists

sneaking a mid-night snack
the 90 degree-ness of the river
a passport and police-badge on
          the sidewalk
kid strung out on heroin
          in the doorway
a picture of Gertrude Stein's grave
my mind a finger I place on
          everything
my touch

—D.D.

Headache again &
sleepy too.
Music just went
off. Reading &
dozing on S.
Paretsky—
"Guardian Angel"
Typed CoLabs today
of B & me.

Lonely.

ok
so
what's the form
to get rid of a
headache
Wren breath
a la mode
Darkness presto!

—L.A.B.

ore

below their face is another surface
only slimmer.
can open wide the door. and supple
sidle the past right tilts in.

she's an ornery so and so and won't

hear none of it.
like lightbulbs, only dimmer.
if we could see the indescribable.
or 3 immutable lies.
(last line)
can see it but can't describe, can't
fasten.

sweetness waiting inexplicably in layers as
the hostess charms from the waist up and refutes

the sky which gets on you no matter
what.

you can berate the weather to death, it doesn't
matter.

a coil of wire tightly stifles. an excuse
nobody asked for, a road cut into

the side of a mountain.

3 shooting stars and then unasked one
horizontal more.

—J.H.

bob dole, mispronounces words, party of the government,
it is demeaning, why now of all times do I have to
think about intelligent people saying stupid things?
to be exact, dwight gooden, looks weird, guess i've never
seen him without his uniform on. rene russo,
bob dole, the baldwin brothers! sherri sylvester,
jack kevorkian, deborah meeks, anthony conti,
hurt in a catastrophe? bob dole, mike kaczmarek,
marilyn whirlwind, everything comes double like sisters
and/or brothers, the brother, greek characters, heart of darkness,
nicholas roeg, larry king.
mike tyson, raymond sierra.

—B.M.

August 16

The impact of this
    is insignificant
how we collide and bounce
   move around
      avoid
human contact I just
want to tell you the truth
you are far back in line
hundreds have come before you

and for this alone I
   apologize my
      attention spans
house of brick and mortar
children inside lapping

He wrote: the sexual
   experience was part
of growing up in my home
: loving mother and naked
and willing body

I somehow did not
think to cringe my
own grievances tearing
   you silent
Cold breakfast a
   kiss on the forehead
red turtleneck sweater new
   to me only because I
have not known you
in winter months   un-
returned phone calls &
   messages   gives
me a little of my own silence
   back but see
I am not occupied with this
   space in the same way
I have my obligations &
 take them with me in dreams
they are dinosaurs
compared to   our last
   encounters a
sudden emotional rift 4 nights
of love-making what
drifts   I have made
    known
open book   I
   laid waste my cage
you can't hurt me
easy come   easy
    go

10 Directions:

Staring across the bar
at your cool exterior
the man behind the counter
   a visit
   I wanted to touch from a
   love-in-question

He maneuvered his mouth so
our lips would meet
      I promised to slap
      him if he got physical
He made tea and went upstairs
      We talked about the surreal quality of
      Mt. Rushmore
Spending the night in his
embrace as friend as rain
as fellow travelers
   a personal ad
   his poem that segued into
   questioning his ex-lovers poetry
   motivation
   that collapses mind
      matures affection
And I loved him for his work
      how he could
turn on a thought
I'm melting
where's the embrace

                         —D.D.

blue corner

the way the violent sky buttons over itself

or hanging in blue uncornered sheets, sheaths, eveless

harpsichords of light, ribs, uncareful apertures

which, once opened, once broke, stiff-jawed and unadvised

as the white-noosed hawk, scaffolding skyward, arpeggios down

as if haste and abandon, need like a rust-ruby turret casting

the blue day behind starting, in fits

—J.H.

Daytime
during concert
Painting—
leave spaces for
words in common

(circular drawing)

after reading **Lag** in *The Black Debt* by Steve McCaffrey
given to me today by Rod Smith

Gal

Rod is a door or adored red, backwards Peugeot is Toeguep,
tomorrow the black slipper cats with be anesthetized and worse, or
should I say today, Gabe sang Hard Times Come Again No More,
we live near Ives Street, "the stars as they publish the clouds from
France," form is found is not yet there, some friend's parents beat a
hasty retreat, in addition to fitting the work already done into some
semblance of a context, coaxed into yet a little bit more work, cats
scale the file cabinet, the act of arranging a room in one's mind,
something to "fall back on", though it's not a novel, tom or row,
upside your head, root gulp or seizure, the drawing of curvilinear
Lee Ann balancing briefly in the physical, Rosmarie advise, the
Djerrasic Foundation borders on Neil Young's zebra farm and dog
school, regular money suggestion produces silence, a pastry filled

with spinach and cheese, codex xerox, just a quilt of thinking, a crumpet banknote means you might get a pet means you might get a rat in your box, keep that towel around your waste, ted debt, deb debt too, walking down the street buying things along the way, a border fiver, blue corn necklace in the sun, pink sherbet tights, boy poems a la mode, innocent enough, the cult of youth is insidious, barbecue forbidden to multiply on prior slopes of blue girls, command apple, no duplication, though the voice bounced and floated, the high notes ease into our drive up and down one ionized pants legs of the rhizomboid jeans with the Willis-Gizzis, negotiating the dream versus everyday verses, fellow Southerner, keep canning

—L.A.B.

czestovona or something like that
will ackerman, biakabatuka
that german was GAY

X FILES EUDORA WELTY

xfiles mrs fest schrift
quantum leap 110 pieces fishing set of hooks
lost the battle lost the war
who the hell is this john ash?

i see so many strange things
big small mouth bass brought to completion

stemmed to completion
fishing system weights rattles hooks free videos

frr frogs
why is my sister so mean to me, is it genetic sibling rivlary and who cares? it would be best not to care about anyone or thing! goodby forever

—B.M.

August 17

how quickly some place can
get used to you
I don't even look up anymore
for lack of surprise   it's not
ownership it's mundanity when
motions past the same angels
in the architecture lack
spark   how easily it is we
forget to be wide-eyed
            until a piece of our past
catches up — ho ho! And
we connect the driving
forces and say yes, I have
another life — like a star trek episode
            Jean Luc Picard almost
            dies in surgery, lives a
            complete life in the meantime
             only to wake up to remember
            he's somebody else
what a gyp, my ex-husband said
I was secretly shocked — to
            be given such an opportunity
            for 2 lives and recall both?
According to aura law we are
attracted to each other's magentas
out here   what makes us
stray from the farm makes
this hodge-podge of weary
travelers my family   what
in the end brought me
enough peace so that I
could return home.

—D.D.

serrations of sky and sky making
shifts in the music so the blue
will break through or lying
in a different position to scatter
the dream

dispersal
on rollerskates hums
a different distant
tune and the phantom
logic of
in sedimentary layers
quarantine suspends
both belief and disbelief

the clouds are dramatic
the clouds are distinct
the clouds are not clouds
is it dumb to write about clouds?
the clouds are chrysanthemum
the clouds in pieces
in fragile redundancy with no running water
methods
of attainment fail
to pronounce
the consonant and i
pick up the phone
anyway disregarding
various considerations and what
my mother would have
me call reality

it would be
true to say
i am left-handed

and i am left-handed

distinction falters haze
systole diastole and vent

the horizon is only itself
and wide wood makes mirrors
undo the dream of dream and sky

—J.H.

Let me explain

A bud or pod colored green and purple emerges
from its layered water nest
under the falls which are directed
without thinking
to be poured onto
or more likely fallen onto
hard
vibratory sections or progressions
towards more than one
or a singular state of fixity
which is actually moving
at an infinitesimal rhythm
airing and lashing each
pointed wray remembers this
that's never this way before

—L.A.B.

August 18

inevitably

variants transcend invitations
moralist misbehavior and i don't
know how not to do it.
a quick list or light. corners.
steps beckon or browse and
flickers pulse and flick leaving
room for critique if necessary.

another view in diagonal
frames to the side with pause
and ill upwards snowy and
plans to run to the store

p.s.   an x
         a star
         a single point
         a stair
         a strife
         a stop in the morning

—J.H.

tonight everyone will write
about the full moon

      everyone will look to the moon
      muse for guidance and inspiration
sky lit and waiting sounds
silenced earth working its way home
      crashing her lost souls
      I
I don't need to see to
know this is true it is so ancient
it was written long ago
      I walked in the door at 12:15
every light was out   I drank water
and St. John's Wort picked up my pad
four hours of climbing scratches on wrists
arms legs satisfied w/a days
work.   Miracles of life: zygote into
ruptured cunt skin
        traveling thru the
urethra the 10 million sperm
           you
were there we all were
collective semen consciousness

and the woman's body attacks these
foreign substances takes em out
one by one.   fifty left.
Day drops down.

books marbles paper planet
ends where?
in a sickening fellow cancer

—D.D.

Conk, (A Flawed Piece) or Flog a Conked Frog
for Roger Williams, Yo-Yo Man & Charlie B.

And though witchs meet under my bookcase
Uncle A said, "No!"
& Further, these Firsts evaporate volatile secretions
that movie when the Johnny Bug Show was mistaken for a
week, rest, rune, ruse rock erase related, no flowed
upwards of the free loaders where B-E-E-T-S not B-E-A-T-S
or just cuz Zukofsky was living off Planet Street
vastly composite (lick lick)—that
stuff yer jonesing for on some kind of
flat, level, slightly elevated surface
time misses
Miss "I do this, I do that," tincture of
Venus Transit meant this:
Virtual Furnace Luck
from Johnson City, Tennessee the lemonade
felt
enveloping the emergencies
attention span web brew of
atonic plethora maps
span paws sawn long
in a bird's barrel—some sloping I
didn't know any better so
reflex and Family bear equals
fabulous night shutting off
to play to become you struggling & soapy changing

O you need to fix it up, ticket-wise
rattling truth womb, these
some men new coloratura repossession manual
Fell or
Lambs eat what?
Stout ouch means more love
voltage
Oracular Okra
Palais
the church of
recoups
avuncular—
well,
what's the aunt?

BEAMISH

I can read
        Frank Lloyd Wright
I can read
        Frank while you write

 Cracks appear in
my parlor
  tender feeling why so
  shy?
past hurt
Tiredness of futile
But the human body is
so beautiful
 A beautiful waltz
Why troubling? Why tired
  & sad?
Having been hurt & tense
Having been alone &
  liking it.
Having gotten carried
        away
not regretting but
more careful

of time left
 I ordered the Pro Jo
for the want ads
Peerless kitchen dance
freeing my October
10:30 1952
you long exotic
 thumbnail
getting allergic to y'all
rubbing yourselves all
over my bed
think big
     he said.
I was I thought.
Where the action is
found this dress on the
street with about
8 others-finally
wearing it after 8
washings & storage-
How strange to see a
pair of shoes in a
public space

                                        —L.A.B.

August 19

olfactory friends: melanuka
     fixer, dektol, refried beans
ivory soap images we
     develop w/our noses   clean
the roots engulf us in our
contrasts   bark covered, strangle

     Triangular mountain view

in six shades of black & white
bells on the cat-collar
Charlie Brown, Led Zeppelin, & those
crazy vinyl 45's,   sleeping
bags spread eagle on the
pool table   empty muffin cup on the
round wooden table of the quiet coffee
shop   butcher shop (this is only an
ear image) w/ a body on the floor bleeding
bag lady w/ a lottery ticket   a woman
traces her footsteps due to her
amnesia   green 3-toed foot
lands in a puddle   tie dye shirts
in the bathtub that leave blue water
soaking   too
   many hours in a dark
room   1 hour on the freeway a
3-day novel   alarm set for 6:30 am
Sunday paper & a new BIG screen
TV theme from Star Wars as I
back out of the driveway

                              Dusk
a bonfire under the chilly stars to
the tune of old Journey songs

   Images too many to count   fade

embers   emit a glow

                                        —D.D.

Light cotton dress folds
under my tongue
as I radially commit

to freeformgroupies

Can't stop singing the weather

76

High up reach my ouch tongue
Moral fiber trusts us not to spill
our guests even though they're
working it out in the bedroom

More or less not apologizing
submitting to eaves or leaves

Aching and writing anyway
Again rose selavie
my bunker is your bunker

—L.A.B.

Not responsible student

whatever adults more complicated.

Some urine jars. When a body

enters into its own summers.

Flagrantly besting.

Migrants don't exist.

or margins.

Footsteps aren't reassuring.

One final disaster-

How offensive money

non-dairy creamer-it's

important to break inside

—J.H.

surrounded by mosquitoes
stung by bees or hornets
at odds with everyone even myself
with so many things that can't be said
unable to finish or begin
i count tiny little accretions in understanding
nobody can understand me
i remember no dreams
it gets worse instead of better
what could be worse
i can't think of anything

i hate you i hate myself i'm paranoid
like i'm too paranoid to say who
i can't see i can't cross the street
i can see, everybody thinks i can cross the street
i have a salamander planes seem to crash
everytime   i think something's good it's bad
my expectations — forget it

people who don't know me can't tell
that it's hard to talk
it says something underneath at least
i don't see snow anymore
                          (who cares who won the winston cup?)

(a glass vase full of tongues)

explication of my recent work

a long time ago, suffering from a summer cold, i lay
down upon a bed of shadows that fell upon me like
prunes, and it struck me that all lives end this way or
that, and that naturally as flowers, we must accept this
as we accept all renewal. this is not without hamstrung portent
however, for just as we accept renewal, we are staggered
with the use of patches. word play brought me from patches
to afro-picks, and the rest just wrote itself.
the works underwent a multitude of revisions before
it found it's vinyl form, and the abject voice which beweeps

the cast of men's fate all too often in this industrial
manic age.

addendum

a number of learned correspondents have quibbled with my
reliance on word play to explain my move away from patches.
perhaps the following, written when i was a mere 40 years of age,
will help to clarify:

> O! thy green jello
>   as sexy as birds
>   of red
>   weedy patches pick
>   african violets
>   plucking a pizzicato
>   piccolo

—B.M.

August 20

bells and whistles, balls and chains, sweets and sugars,
levitation, leviathons, huckleberries, loss of
memory, loss of visions, court stenographers,
lilies, day lilies, days, dailies, princes, flocks,
linings, organs, pedal pushers, illustrious
critiques and declarations
farther out along the
smaller than previously
made of stone with air
formerly contained pier
gingerly and sadly
windy while fishing
awoke untamable
began to run

arrival in a field of
usurpation aftermath
and this without thinking
jams and preserves
without thinking much less do i waver
or travel vouchers under
a stiff sun
the body circulates freely
in a field of constraint
clothed or unconcerned
first to burst, then to flee
failed remedies or remedies
not sought and an encounter
in a dim clean afternoon
now awaits or dream life unwaveringly curtailed.

—J.H.

for Alison Dorfman

    Once in a while you
meet a great   mind who
tells you of a place

the place is yours, you
only need to learn how
to get there

maybe my luck is changing.
I had a visit from the bad
Karma fairy this week.

Downhill   is the direction
I went rapidly
               Too
hot in August to be
worrying about money.

—D.D.

today somebody said it was september but
it wasn't the landlord, i dreamed
silver tongues came to rest on german children
and pink and green mountains erupted
in the middle of the cafe gigi where we ate
purple plums till we were blue in the face
and died of bleeding ulcers on avenue a
            i
then we saw a green couch on the corner
and sat down and ate a moon and cheese sandwhich

to which i added a yellow tomato dipped in
honey mustard dressing made palatable by electrical
systems built during the snows of jupiter which took place
when the great white father, i can't remember what
he did. see you later.

                        s
skunk saviour
            ss
                    german ss secret service?

                                —B.M.

Echinacea tingle, a
book on Rocky Mountain
Wildflowers on the bathroom floor.
Marie & Soph come in
looking radiant. Soph is
doing that great arguing
that a daughter does
for her mother — wanting
her to have fun instead
of being so responsible
There is a flower
    called Sky Pilot
which favors disturbed

soils along roads. It's grown in "gopher
gardens"—and is called
skunkweed too.
There is a picture of S.
in the paper I haven't
seen yet—been apart
1 week and 1/2 — it would
be a picture of him taken
since I've seen him
Am I fat partly because I'm
on the pill? I think
maybe so. Will my body
lose this habit if I stop?
I was happier at,
more relieved (?) at passing
my damn typing test
40 wpm than I was at
graduation.
Side backache
tired. blue
flannel sheets & indian
no andean?
blanket wind keeps blowing
the door open.
Lambert is Loco
  crazyweed?
   locoweed
     extremely
  showy
Bernadette is writing in
the kitchen. Food Stamp
Goat cheese for dinner.
Met "Andre Quo-Vadis"
at Bonanza busstop today.
Saw "Toys" on the
little green then pink
tinted screen.
Sent letters to M. Harper,
Margie Keller—finally
passed my mandatory 40 wpm typing test after

10 tries—
I usually compose
out of my head—
but no wonder it takes me
so long to type other people's
manuscripts
   Bad habits.
Must be more focused.
Cleaned house for
Ben F., Kristin Prev.
& Alan G. to stay in.
I keep singing
Chorus Line—
O god I need this job
Bob Holman teaching
2 classes at New
School—B only one
& not included in
their NY Times Ad.
Don't know what
they've got access
to— says they think she's the one
"who teaches old people"
Skyrocket or Fairy Tripod
attracts hummingbirds also called
Polecat Plant—upper leaves
give off skunklike smell
when crushed.
Snowball Saxifrage?

                              —L.A.B.

August 21

FANTASTIC AS THIS:

> we trying to get back
> to each other

And this is Venus in her full day
facing front and center
never have I seen her in such glory
shining orange blue yellow

holds her breath and turns colors for us
as the world unquiets itself
paying you no attention
> filling itself with warmed-up
American Dream
> Efforts to infect you
> sobering, as best done is
capturing the flag and bringing home moment
[been there, done that, bought the software]

more on the weekends
fending our elbow room
private guest teams
burglar-proofed windows
x-ed in the right places
the punishments never enough
time blurring the edges
sneaking out the back door
Venus you move so fast
> faster inside of me
> as time becomes inconsequential
our mascots such painful reminders of
> ignorance
our ignorance a painful reminder of
> our mortality
our mortality a painful reminder

                of our futility
So shall we keep our mascots or
                create purpose in them?
Now behind the clouds   Venus waits

        Here comes the sun.

                                —D.D.

because evrything seemed trivial
(northern exposure was almost over)
russell said he would leave me a note
(we decided phil must take ecstasy)
outlining his new sense of clarity
we decided marie might have to get it for us at the lime light)
which he was pretty sure he would have in the morning
(i had watched a program about a dying body causing every
body in the emergency room to get sick)
& i told him i'd be dazzled by the truth just like
emily dickinson
(now phil's awake watching three's company)
& i'm dying for the note

                                —B.M.

owe

                        mismo   same
                        same   mismo
was going to be
                        a description
    a same treatise
                        on tardiness and
        bickering the shape out of
        an evening

                    fabric in distress
        fallen
            from grace or intent
            the girdle of language
which holds you up
in rhythm
which lets you down
                        gently or not gently
                        coming unfastened quickly
        in recognition, in time, in fits
        and starts falling like held
        breath in hushes over the sleepless
        organizations of light

2.   sheets of rain

the book closing, thistle
in sensation or color, two
or more differing opinions,
getting drenched in rhythm

four hours later, the night
gets in you more quickly, the damp
in bones entrenched specific or
held gingerly between the teeth

of guilt and the gears of dream
slapping against again and again
why do we do what we do
and the sounds of sleep and subway

the book or bed propped open, reasoned
towards a source of listening
alarms sound uselessly and the objects
of a life placed expendable on a sheet

counting backwards or the aid of introductions
annotated directional to guide the impulse
further into its future what liquid
there is versus what liquid we need

against the surface of a photo
things dissipate in color
so as not to say death versus
all the other reasons a person might

forget or remember or stay asleep
when what is asked is punctual
attention requires no deficit nor debt
yet the thought of all those other months

—J.H.

             Subway
           vibration
         missing or skipping
something that's supposed to
happen in a house just
_____with my lamps & beds
"scared the living daylights
out of me"
I stood on the
platform
feeling the slightest
turn-on as the
mechanical hum of
the subway & the way
people were moving
vibrated ever so
fascinatingly
in my being
all different kinds of people

—L.A.B.

August 22

two-fisted compliments about
to be heavy it is these things
which affect copyright law
so greatly.

thus did we liven many a
mundaner meal, and thus
did the city get under our
skin.

speaking of sand, the
invitation was written in
bird crumbs and imbalance
ruled, we never got our footing,
nor wanted it, preferring instead to
fall lazily, loosely forward on one foot and fail and
fail to trace our way home.

—J.H.

There was timing and the terrible anger. At first jobs
incorporating hiding in the dark. Then raises consisted of
running, hiding, jumping. One guy's promotion. Then we
might get bored and...Master — We shoot them down we can
shoot them down we lay on top of a moving target. Did he
retire? I'm not sure. We're not sure. He lives there probably. I
just wanted a head to turn. I just wanted to be recognized. I
took over the gurney, the patient covered up but not dead. A
part of the promotion. 2 guys have to agree on it but that
happens rarely. Medium rarely. Love reversal. Banging on the
boardroom door trying to make some sense of things. When you
get there at 3 all your things and luggage will be waiting for you.
Board a train. I could do that. Put a bone on top of my head
and make a decision. We'll be honost w/ her and tell her
probably "no." Then he fell from 20 stories up. He died but still

told his sister, "I fell" she
said, "I don't believe this"

—D.D.

'someday
the children of Odysseus
will kill no more'   —Ed Sanders

Athena
Pronoia
Cassandra at Woodstock

—L.A.B.

August 23

peggy, bob and elizabeth were
hanging out and we were talking
i saw a pack of Kool's and knew
it was a dream from the previous hypnogic
looking at colors, eyes closed, let me put it
another way:
                    i had been trying to be
in this hypnagogic state when i realized
                        close my eyes and
all i had to do was/ look at the strange colors
i could see confusion (it was a visual thing),
then i thought it might be interesting to
experiment with eating — to see if there was
any difference in what i could see if my stomach was
in the processs of digesting. i ate some (what turned
out to be old) cranberry sauce and was in the
process of observing what might happen when i
fell asleep and had the dream about peggy, bob
& elizabeth & the pack of Kools we went to see
"basquiat" today and later rosemary called to say

that bob viscuzi was in the channel 13 little italy
program, and that she was in possession of a letter
i sent her & vito saying why i thought marrying
bob was a bad idea. marie was here with finn, lee
ann was here, max and laura are here, tomorrow i'll go
to olive with phil (& maybe others), tonight we
went to veniero's

—B.M.

　　　seated　or maybe
the cat-bird situation
caught:
　　　feathers in mouth

No matter what I say
　　(no win)
although gentler with myself
　　awake

—D.D.

outlaw

head down　　　　torpor
legally yours
in the warehouse or wondrous
(as if sleep would anywhere else)
has become ordered　　　as if to say
how elderly must we be before
truncated at the what
or why continue when
dear tall you, what gives?
a revelation and then wanting
to go dancing and lapping

at the sidewalk the bay
has moved its chill toes
elsewhere

elements cause sudden wonder
thistles drink more
in a manner of hovering
or needing an order which hand
once held forgets not

as it's never enough
we just collide artfully
in dream lives or clean
house frantically with ill-
derived intentions to please impossibly
plagues impede memory's epidemic
or infected ideology to not say
what we remember
part once more whether desire
mentions or skims of a
membraned network as if
such and such or so and so and elsewise
the windows shatter more stilited
each time the light grains in

—J.H.

"he shld be paid much more for what he's doing"

—L.A.B.

August 24

More sameness sanity in-
can't see moon through window can't think with
Independence effects special my gift to landscape
No genius wonders why things come the way they do
why I have to save a mouse from cats and worry about
its kamikaze from our back deck
why I let the knives pile up
why the TV is such noise
why I read so slow, have to look words over,
chew them so hard and still, still they disappear
think,
verstehen,
ich bin eine Seejungfer
Ich habe in der Meer von Wort geschwummen
hilfreich
hilfreich
die Welle,
die Welle kommen
And how long can I hide
as pampero twists my purpose and
I falter like a leaf in summer
I want to be a mystagogue but have no doctrine
I want to be fine and delicately glazed
but cannot withstand the heat
I want to be a pagan, but don't know who to thank
Empty hallways in dreams turn into supermarkets,
Echoes become phone calls from
well-meaning friends who don't know
when they speak the truth,
wisdom not in the claiming to teach,
wisdom in the letting go

Search, my bones are too hard, my drill not deep enough
when will the ice finally melt and cool
floors become familiar,
past life cats want to know when to purr

when to be a work of art and when
to conceal
lessons are palatial, they prolong mortality
That's it, you know, we only want to be immortal
A colored piece in the mosaic of time
Not to shrivel, be dwarfed in the light of tomorrow,
isolated, erosive, nilled

—D.D.

nausea
comportment
lack
aid to hair
to sleep
hear
now

Gap

or knot
                fist of idea
    ripped into knowledge

any day can begin
                the week or encourage
        time to spin or scatter

    only slightly clean and less vested
        (recessed) risen or chosen
        or changed position

—J. H.

August 25

nature's fury great balls of fire tutti frutti
who'll stop the rain poignant and painful of an era
jesse jackson, for, the whole world is watching
ted sorenson, about hair restoration, nick nolte
there's a mouse eating my jello! i hate you
h.v. kaltenborn a cat kissing a mouse! and they're
playing "silent night" and "jingle bells" while
now it's i don't know what and soon we're going to
emily dickinson's house, tomorrow it's the democratic
convention in chicago janis joplin i wonder if being
tie-dyed or tired is the same as it used to be!
did you read i can't remember what? look it's got stitching
all over the front. today we saw india and bernard's
house plus the outside of the saltbox something — or —
other, you've got mail, this morning we woke up in
woodstock, we were the first to use i can't remember
what, the cat and the mouse are back again, they keep showing
the ancient democratic conventions of chicago, it's
the prelude to the itchy and scratchy show, now the
mouse is blowing up the cat, now an ad for a correspondence
school, i wonder if this is on for my benefit or maz's
now a scissor, now a scissor, now ginger ale, now some natural
saratoga spring water, russell's forgotten his nicorette
gum! it's called the gift of gag, we saw eight million
ways to die based on the lawrence block book with a screen-
play by oliver north (and somebody else), democratic
convention by oliver north (and somebody else)

—B.M.

in the dream everyone spoke very
proper mocking British English & we were
trying to make phone calls to Austria, where
cats & humans alike were

relaxing in the lap of luxury. It was all very
sexual, even the breast-like mountains.
Man tried to convince us to spend our
nights in sex pubs, but we're
disinterested. He's incredulous.

I did walk the night pier & viewed
the lighted castle. Everywhere the
easy laughter of drunk tourists. What's
lacking in the U.S. are places
to walk the streets sans cars &
among cheery coffee houses for people to take
a load off forget the competitive
edge, forget the drive of material advantage,
gain, loss, it's all the same.
Earlier at the baths, older Italian man tries
to show me how to float on spiral jet
stream of water. I can't stay up,
we laugh as I float away, get
water up my nose. Here, at the baths,
the land of dirty looks melts into
folds of skin, hairy backs, see-through
bathing suits. When was the last time I saw
so many people laughing together at
the same joke? Blue sky, concrete
statues, and more folds of skin.
How they can't tuck it all in and
really don't care. This ain't no L.A.
beach scene. These folks alive.
Earlier still I made progress w/ the
cave church & the peace statue — woman w/ leaf
(originally meant to be a sword) stretching
up on top of Gellert Hill before the
citadel. The green of old statues running
down her sides, down the pedestal onto the
steps where I sat to contemplate
my lack of emotional connection w/ Budapest
it may not be my city,
but it's made a point. It's got
wisdom enough to gouge the

tourists to build its economy and
anciently hip enough to keep us all interested.

—D.D.

yet

one more

cannot and do

again again

what makes this

liable   shelter

or not want to

integrate

no passport, no telephone

is worth is worth

ledgers and fans

planned escape

—J.H.

August 26

Sorry the blanks on the
      Sorry the
wall began w/ sorrow clues
      it seems I want to
apologize for somethng, but
         don't know what it is
    too many people mad
at me or is it only
myself
big as I am, and mean,
with terrible ogre voices

that accuse. accuse and
demand things. take no
substitutions, no imitations.
they want prisoners and the
rest of me knows it.

    I saw the mountains

and the red moon,
see them every day.

    saw the sunset light
streaming from the back of

    Long's Peak. saw the storm
clouds ominous creeping
above the Flatirons   the
periodic   flash   of
lightning
    How beautiful I
always thought each time
how beautiful

    So what draws me

away? Makes me want to
leave? Calls Calls Calls
in back of membrane

      to go

      I itch, I scratch
      I get mad, I drink
      I'm sad, I cry
I'm joyful, I laugh
I'm hungry, I eat
      empty, fill myself
I'm loving, I make love
I'm sleepy, I sleep
I'm breathless, I breathe
I'm dirty, I clean
I'm desperate, I   dream
I want to leave
      where do I go?

                —D.D.

deportments

truly ascended
with a companion or mother
it is enough
or it is not enough
as people, seamstresses
not an "issue"
in whatever language

a jar of anise
a jar of arnica
a jar of hair
a jar of eucalyptus

someday it'll be automatic
until then, keep saying it

every day or as needed

cleanliness or automatically
she got up every morning
losing sleeplessness so the thing
articulated the wrong shape
strangely subdued or sensical
numerals suffer to suddenly expand
more or less
something inside which wanted
out or outside which desperate
clamor mistaken for a friendly
hello or inability to be on time

some places we'd never go
though admire the extrerior
of a building or thought build
on a street corner in history
obnoxious over the years or hey,
what can   you do

no wind
no sur
no traffic
not yet
light

—J.H.

been too ill in mind, body, & clock to write

— L.A.B.

here's a box of brass plated steel
escutcheon pins next to the yellow highlighter which
is actually a flourescent marker. tonight i learned
(it's very cow in this house) that not only has every expectation

that a person who wants to change the world might actually
be elected by the majority officially ended but also
people who want to get elected a la democratic convention
seem to be thoughtlessly willing to change
their beliefs to please others and to get their votes plus
they are totally boring there's a guy holding the club!
he looks like the devil, on the day gerard died, gary
who writes all the time but refuses to ever publish his work
broke his key in the club or broke a key in a club, the room
is large the room is large . . . .

turkey hill carrot cake ice cream

—B.M.

August 27

      coyote & dog wails echo the canyon
           like a movie set
I doubled back on the lightning
           crazed road to take picture of
stiff-legged elk
head lopped off for the trophy antlers
Rio Grande canyon walls tell me to
              jump, or rather, let go
                and fly
All I've been doing
           flying one place to next
readying for my photo finish
    washing landscapes with clods
of philosophy
    awkward guesses as to
           what's out there

Rio Grande answers
                      nothing
wide skies sunsets backdrop as I

                continue to move
                air and heat waving to the bone
        even in the rain it feels dryer than home

        as I water the storm up
                        brew and breath
        green river below
        2 ravens riding the wind
        sage and cactus at feet
        flying is easy
        it's the landing gets me down

                                                —D.D.

dole = o.j.

cancer what a downer cancer cancel
highlighter spider

                                                —B.M.

sequential

thinks can't hypnotize
percolate instead on the upswing
memorized in tables, subjects, flair
as below will come a bell or bus
out of whack and so not watching
paying lending formulations of
another former self-made
auto-efficient timing device
as simultaneity is what
you'd call it a cultural virtue
sore in the throat and limbs
the same as ever why some things
never change and others do too

often the door screenless, precarious
available but requiring balance
and in the middle of the discussion
i opened it for her.

—J.H.

August 28

a brief history of zoning

whether you will turn your head or not and

keys fallen to uncertain
demise.

approximate lines incite

partners in crime, or just
partners, or just crime

—J.H.

gibbons decline and fall of the roman empire — what a
downer

a shade of green against a fresh early riser empty chair in a starless
    sky before an unexpected guest listening to crown
the important clock is in the room with us
a wealth of reading material
william clinton is the man from hope and was nominated
a blessing of turquoise/ in front of a stale late bloomer crowded
settee
in a skyless airplane after a hapless visitor watching thrushes
the silly anti-timepiece is not in the osmosis avec vous

since the un-nation stood for not standing for nothing no more we went
for walks and had talks
we took our pleasure in making no promise
    and while many cows across the land turn to meat after school smoking
    is still in fashion
fashion is loving to commit crimes: phil, do you feel that armed robbery,
    for instance, is morally reprehensible?
tell us! is the moon full? is it out? if not full, what stage is it in?
what constellation or other celestial phenomena can you see?
do you like the domocrats or republicans or neither?
do you feel, like mike tyson, that jail is useless?
jail is our public system of turning people into cattle
    I say jailbreak   BREAKOUT
and all issues break out of normal rules found objective
or subjective! jail is dick gephardt, i feel
jail is tipper gore! oh save me from watching more of the demo-cratic
convention, politics is
forget it! let's have our own party
the Bernadette Mayer party
the truth food sex and poetry party
the constellations party, we won't have anybody speaking
who has a relative who's died; (somebody just said, 'no man
is an island' — uh oh the value of it all
just another speaker saying the same old you know the same old
tune? the sky is the limit to which only when the full moon sets
do the stars come out along with the meat flavored cat foods
and birch bayh's son had twins and they eat american baby food
from a jar and
last year america built more cars and this poem has gone to far and
look there are pineapples on the wall paper and i'll say!

                              —B.M.

Very body conscious
   at 'home' (NC)
an ear folded over
Days lost-
   no subconscious
"it's just too painful"
In morning mourning
   still in mourning
Wanted to claim(?)
an embrace _____
Blurry shaking
only relax when decision
is made
Uptown in Mary Duncan's
dress w/out a slip.
Met Carolyn-Ruth
Grier's daughter-
off to beach
tomorrow on HiWay 74
where Michael Jordan's
      dad was just killed

With Jennifer!
My childhood friend
"Gotta just
rely on
yourself"

Fish oil
food as comfort &
stimulation,
later burden
I shake my
upper arms
Moments graphed on
the wall-
JFG sign
      Diana by Anna
Hyatt Huntington
the DIAMOND

restaurant shines
in the night
my father's office
presented as darling-
up high
  old ladies shoot baskets to
while Beach Music
loud in pink
shirts
step kicking a
white filling on
the back
rice w/
Mushrooms & Chicken
  broth
"asparagrus"
  salmon
Noah's long dark lashes

                                        —L.A.B.

August 29

berry picking @ dusk

Snap of branches turns head
hoof beats and hoots
smear over-ripeness into bucket
hand caught in spider web
sandals through grass dew
    the feet
Flying ants shed wings
on fall sweater, swat away the
    remaining bodies
Swarms of mosquitoes bite
    through clothes
            more branches, fur

& tracks on trail
Bring the berries in, consider a   rest
Consider the subtle white blue sky
Consider the voice box making
    stories into tears
Consider the snake under the
    door jamb, tucked into
    a plastic garbage can &
    let into the wilderness
        sans cats
Consider silhouette-trees
    sharp black edges
    under plane screech
I don't consider this easy
    consider it one-sided
Don't consider.

—D.D.

Hurricane
    Emily
Anthem for
    Mixed
    Voices

Running
Exercising
while
Intoxicated

Shift
a figure in one
there are butterfly
farms
A blurry figure
on the beach

peach blanket
wearing a shift
very dark &
swollen with cold ?
Heavy humidity
nostalgia salt
gathers on my
skin
a cricket shift
cuddle many our
            self
encouraged to groom

A pea rcy
    cent

B Stravinsky
   looking real
            serious

Full moon
   approach

Proetry
   so we can
Sale them

            Willy Wonka &
the Chocolate Factory

                                —L.A.B.

parties, communist and otherwise

there is no brief history.
the light is striated and unthinkable.
a sink is a quiet moment before a fall.
a quiet motion.

no cure for thirst.

as if water might
just fall from the sky

as if the sky itself

                                          —J.H.

is the amethyst rock more important than the clock?
john kennedy toole, j cortaghession boyle,
jackie kersee-joyner, maybe it's corraghessian boyle,
or doyle or dole, reduced juice, reduced juicer,
who what when where how which disease?
how many women get aids? how many women don't get aids?
if something has to be wrong, you can either be all
fucked up to begin with or become that way later, that is,
you can only function because your all fucked up or
you can only function if your fucked up in some way — you
get my meaning? how many women get tested for aids?
are you considered sick if you have _____?

what diseases can you have without being considered
sick? is _____ a disease? you wrote the book on

sensitivity, didn't you? amen.   rita dove

                                          —B.M.

August 30

No one here—
        The calm before
the storm— out of bed &
onto the beach—warm
water almost full

moon Jennifer
down the beach with
Cathy with a C—
I turn of the bad
music inside it
takes a while for
the tv to go away along
with the pain in my
neck
what I want
is
independance
strength
intimacy
security   strong
indentities
Ability
developed
poetic risk
brushing ever (?)
up for 10
   more minutes
What dream it's gone
Lonely now especially
because of cultural
rift— set myself
apart— but not
much in common—
will I write a song
common for "any"one
is there a song for "any"one
the clouds are
wisps in circular drifts
clear around the
stars—
She broke my date—
(well he broke more than that)
when will I learn to
cease to be disapppointed
the way things happen—

hard to get together
a miracle if you
do
not a given
the little sad birds
are still going at it despite
the night—by the dark
shine of the almost full
moon

—L.A.B.

almost letting go
                rush of skin   over   tongue
                    down back of throat
            my degree comes in handy
                in solitiude

Sisters,
        forgive something
Thank you once again for the
                journey
            for the task at hand
                under foot
was circumscribing your
            own painful news

save the drop
        cascade
            sweat
all the way down
        the
        page
    body   bag

—D.D.

it is the radical wish-list of the education-cutting,
environment trashing, medicare-slashing, choice-denying,
tolerance-repudiating, gay-bashing, social security-threatening,
assualt rifle-coddling, government-closing, tax loophole-granting,
minimun wage-opposing, republican majority that dominated the
delegations in san diego.   - -ted kennedy
tatterdemalion, origin unknown, oh you mean that wildflower thing
i wish i wasn't back where i started from, everyone's gone (to bed
except me and marie who's asleep on the couch and whoever's
awake in the children's room (there's some music on; they're not
really children)); i give up, i've succumbed to t/v/ and disasters,
i forget what else, now everybody's moving around, now almost
everybody's gone, who is in the kitchen? there is/was a giant
cockroach in the kitchen but nobody'll ever know it. i think that i
shall never see a poem as lovely as a tree! i wish it weren't so,
now it's time to write something . . i take that back! exclamation
points are as frequent as deja vus, i mean the desire to use
exclamation points frequently is beginning to seem like the
neurological problem of experiencing frequent deja vus, even
when they don't seem to be appropriate.

northern exposure seems to have ended.
the means of _____
enforced blindness

                                             —B.M.

notes towards

wheezes and spins

calming into space

acquisitive heaving

full of emptiness or

emptiness leaving

before it's due

—J.H.

August 31

The new & old converse
and disperse   the
surrounded by air and See
everything has become a garden
even the rocks have learned
how to bathe in *die Sonne*
Sonnenblume the only
German name for a flower
that I know. always
wanting to know more, my own
Garten.
Love takes its
strange place in the way
humans help each other.
I don't understand the
word hate. Semantics is a
weedy garden. No one wants
to trim it. Who knows where
it gets its water.   Love
can live a long time w/out sun.
But in the end.
         I'm full
of cliches. I'm full of
you. I refused to be confused
or side-swiped. I throw
stones. I eat stones. I
build, crash down, rebuild.
in the city of style, I wait
underneath the style, wait as
protection against my own self.
Wave my hand. Take the

112

next pill. Roll over. Be me
for a while. Step out. Be you
for a while. Be afraid that
eventually the time & money
will run-out

A man painting the sidewalk w/
crayons.
        His portrait amazingly
flawless & colorful. I worried
        for the both of us about
rain. I would've stayed all day if I weren't
living together already
Collect those feathers. Collect
those eggs.
        Some you have to see this
way, others you have to sing

—D.D.

driven or

alone we

are required

to approve

only the

three

candles the

doctors find,

near the

fan's even

toltec

pintes,

i know them

fourteen

per limp as we hear what

we didn't want to.

—B.M.

Pressed

the last or not the last
            passed
    by calling and otherwise
not knowing
        sweetly
        or sometimes sweetly

after the passageway
followed another passageway
                vocally present
        the hypno element
                became woozy
or in the attempt lay the failure
        and vice
or plausibly on the same day
                street or plane

softly saltily hidden away

if i were bernadette i might tell you

a bit about tomorrow and history plus
a real sexy description of a curb
and curving away but instead i'm
me in the midst of being me
on a red sheet

a friendly month has passed
                limpid violet
then the music swelled
                        then car alarms

                *

moment: un minuto mas

the day spins out of idea
time framed by prior agreement
an interior space spinning
pinging quiet and raw into another
moment, another body, another
time por favor

                                —J.H.